DO I HAV NARCISSISTIC PERSONALITY?

What is a narcissistic personality disorder, how to identify a narcissist, why people become narcissistic, and how to overcome narcissism

DR. ELENORA DAVIS I

CONTENTS

CHAPTER ONE

Introduction

How would you describe a narcissist?

Narcissists have a tremendous sense of their importance and a strong need to be respected and thought of, making them hard to treat.

Self-absorption, or narcissism, is built on a lack of confidence, even though narcissists often seem very sure of themselves. This person acts incredibly rudely because they feel like they don't belong.

The three main types of narcissism are as follows:

There three types of narcissists: the grandiose "overt," the weak "cover," and the high-functioning "exhibitionist."

Typically, when you think of a narcissist, you imagine the overtone. Because of this, they are narcissistic and may act more mean to get your attention and get you to do what they want.

On the other hand, the covert narcissist might come off as one. They should be the main focus of attention, yet they might make an unforeseen request for it. For instance, if you cross them, you can get the silent treatment to encourage you to comply with their wants and requirements. This type may be defenseless against scrutiny and intensely preoccupied with their perceived setbacks, yet they also have an underlying sense of dominance.

The exhibitionist narcissist comes into play at this point. This kind may come out as confident and booming, but it's all just a show of their inner self-reliability. If you were at a posh café, they might brag about how well they know the wine list, and you might find it alluring right away, but they're just trying to make you feel inferior.

Whenever you work with a narcissist, regardless of the sort, you frequently feel unnoticed and downright repulsive.

Narcissistic behaviors in a relationship

It's prevalent for narcissists to love-bomb their spouse at the beginning of a relationship to draw them in and start the abuse cycle. You might believe you've met the world's most intelligent person if they send you flowers weekly and message you all day. They are currently controlling you by just reflecting on your compassionate demeanor.

Gaslighting is another typical narcissistic behavior. Narcissists gaslight because their self-image is so weak that they cannot recover if they are genuinely at fault; therefore, they cause people to put the responsibility back on themselves. A narcissist apologizing: "Drop it. They don't apologize because doing so would be an admission of their flaws.

As a result, narcissists usually have a past full of devoured connections because it is either how they operate or how they choose to remember the past.

Furthermore, you may start to recognize the following patterns of behavior, risks, and other oppressive features, such as controlling the story, after a narcissist can no longer deceive or dominate you. They will ensure that everyone who knows you two acknowledges that you are causing these problems. Since they cannot accept rejection, they can exact revenge in silly and seriously terrifying ways.

Relationships between narcissists and their partners are harmful.

Understanding how a narcissist thinks might help them relax, whether or not they want to damage their partners.

- Relationships with narcissists are challenging to maintain.

4

- They are incredibly flimsy and sensitive so they can whine with no issues.
- As a result, couples may repeatedly fight about the same issues.
- They occasionally lack knowledge of the oppression of their partners, yet sometimes they will need to harm them.
- Finally, as their partner, you must decide if the challenging task will be worthwhile for you in the long run.

If you are involved with a narcissist, you have likely been on a wild roller coaster of good and bad moments.

Everything would have been lovely at first. You might have even believed you had found the ideal spouse. However, sooner or later, everything started to go south.

This is due to the narcissist's Inability to find any value in you after a few weeks, months, or even years. When people realize you are a natural person and hence flawed, they struggle to perceive your value any longer. They'll start blaming you for things, yelling at you, or even breaking up with you. They'll pass on you to mend whatever went wrong.

But it can be challenging to determine whether narcissists want to cause harm to others for a variety of reasons.

Narcissists are easily offended by things.

Narcissists are exceedingly unsteady and self-defensive. They keep their radio wire out if someone ignores them or takes anything from them. You have a wide range of susceptible people that require compassion since, for whatever reason, they don't feel awful when you feel awful and can harm you covertly.

Despite this, hurting a narcissist's feelings is not a difficult task. Due to their incredible responsiveness, they see anything their spouse says or does as an attack. Any situation in which they are not their partner's center presents a significant challenge for them.

You're witnessing someone who is ludicrously unreliable and lacks genuine internal confidence on which they can rely. They rely on external validation.

Narcissist isn't getting what they need without constant approval from their partner, so they look for it elsewhere. As a result, many egotists frequently end up lying.

Narcissists are capable of doing something utterly awful in a second. They say things many people would struggle to speak to someone they love. This is a direct effect of something called "object stability," according to many.

Object stability refers to the ability to consider the entire relationship if someone does something that demoralizes you.

As a result, there are no memories of the fun moments in the narcissist's head while they are ranting at you for something they believe you did. They are experiencing life as a single angry moment with you. They genuinely can't stand you at that point.

The minor lines do twist crazily.

Whether in a relationship with a narcissist or not, relationships are complicated.t. Every pair has been pushed to investigate the various difficulties of cohabiting. But when the person you are with continuously believes they are the one in question, those regular disputes become even more severe and relationship-crushing. This makes even tiny disagreements grow into full-blown fights, harming the narcissist's relationship.

I observe women in the group I trained who have grown to be restless and sad and whose capacity for work has diminished. Because the person kept coming at them and had no guards, they had fits of fear, and one of them was hallucinating and suspicious.

Narcissists may occasionally mean no harm to you. Their brains are wired to be extremely sensitive to everything. Additionally, they will bite back much harder if they believe—according to their logic—that they are being sought after.

However, given their personality, they can also feel the need to harm you because it makes them feel in charge.

It would be ideal if you decided on the relationship's value.

Because the results are usually relatively similar, it doesn't always make sense to address what they are expecting. People who associate with narcissists frequently find themselves engulfed in the same arguments. This is commonly followed by punishment, which, depending on the type of narcissist they are with, may take the form of a heated confrontation or a relaxed, calm approach.

Eventually, being in a relationship with a narcissist drains you, and no matter how long you are together, you must accept that they will never comprehend how you feel. Some people may learn how to be conscious and recognize when they are hurting them over time. This does not guarantee they won't object, though.

Because they are so susceptible, lack empathy, and have poor object stability, narcissists are ready to commit harm. Therefore, they are willing to gripe, misbehave, and lack comprehension. For a partner who is not narcissistic, it is a lot of work.

CHAPTER TWO

The reasons for narcissists' behavior are unclear.

Narcissists lack or have a weak sense of self. They possess a unique way of thinking and being compared to others. Whether due to nurture or nature, they behave the way they do because of how their brains are wired.

The Actual Cause of Narcissistic Behavior

Traditional narcissistic behaviors include:

- Taking advantage of others without acknowledging wrongdoing.
- Needing constant praise.
- Displaying a propensity toward selfishness.

Another review reveals that narcissists behave in such a way out of weakness rather than because they are overflowing with self-absorption.

People with these tendencies control their low self-esteem by acting in standard narcissistic ways.

These include exploiting others without responsibility, needing constant praise, and displaying a penchant for narcissism and bombastic grandiosity.

Unfortunately for narcissists, these behaviors eventually lead to others disliking them, irritating their poor self-esteem.

What does a narcissist require in a partner?

Narcissists are incredibly complex creatures. From one perspective, they can be so intensely self-absorbed that you believe they are unaware of you, and from another, they can be so gravely inundating you with love that you are unsure of how you can ever get away from them.

What exactly does a narcissist require in a partnership with such hot and cold personalities?

This is the simple and direct answer. They require someone who will do all it takes to support them. That will occasionally imply that they need a ton of praise and gratitude from you.

They occasionally need to relax in an ideal relationship where the drug-like enchantment they experience at the beginning of a relationship lasts forever. Unfortunately, all good connections require work, and they don't need that relationship.

Narcissists typically seek a specific type of spouse. They require a person who is adaptable, unquestioning, and susceptible to their manipulations.

No matter how they treat their partner, they need someone who will always make them feel powerful and support them.

If you are involved with a narcissist, you might wonder what qualities about you drew them to you. Some of the excellent traits narcissists look for in a partner include the ones listed below.

#1 Continuity

The majority of narcissists require a devoted partner. They must believe you genuinely have their best interests at heart. Unfortunately, their steadfastness only leads in one way. Therefore they need a partner who can put up with an unpleasant relationship.

Rarely do narcissistic partners feel the need to demonstrate stability. They're ready to get rid of you and move on to another accomplice once they've extracted as much from a relationship.

#2 Someone Who Isn't Inquisitive

The narcissist's inner self is unbelievably fragile and is not amenable to scrutiny. They could live without having their motivations for acting a certain way or having their emotions scrutinized.

Narcissists think they have the chance to do and say anything they want without experiencing too many negative consequences.

#3 A Lack of Self-Esteem

Narcissists need someone loyal to them and who they can influence at all times. A low-confidence cooperator would be easier to manage and probably wouldn't possess the high-status qualities they seek.

High-confidence partners are more eager to demand self-absorbed supply because they will not put up with the narcissist's self-image.

The narcissist searches out someone with fragile self-confidence; they must look to be incredibly wealthy on the surface but be unreliable and easily hurt on the inside. Narcissists focus on these flaws when more inventory is needed and utilize them as tension points.

#4 Feelings of Guilt

When something isn't their fault, some people often feel remorse. They repeatedly review the events, looking for any mistakes that might have contributed to the undesirable outcome. They frequently have no accountability for their development and no power to change it.

Narcissists use that accountability to their advantage by turning any criticism or difficulty in their relationship into something to feel guilty about. If you call the narcissist out for being terrible or manipulative, they may respond by claiming that you never appreciate everything they have done for the relationship.

#5 Compassion

Compassionate people believe they may experience their partner's emotions as if they were their own. This increases the number of people they can quickly grab and gives them more control over those around them.

Narcissists use emotional displays to gain control; if they think someone should be upset with them, they pretend to be bothered by putting on a distressed expression, even if it isn't how they feel.

#6 Someone who feels accountable to others

Narcissists appear to have an inflated self-image, yet it is fragile and requires constant, careful maintenance. When they need a boost of encouragement, they need a companion who will comfort them and boost their self-esteem.

When their partner is in charge of that understanding of specific expectations, those who feel a strong sense of obligation toward others will go out of their way to support their relationship.

#7 High Status

An egotist needs the opportunity to elevate their status, and having a partner with a high level is a fantastic way to do so.

They won't be interested in a spouse with a more excellent status than they do because it would make them look bad.

The ideal companion is someone of equal status, and they can later downgrade that decision if they ever appear to be in a position to surpass the narcissist in prestige.

#8 Someone Who Will Put Their Needs Aside

Narcissistic spouses require someone who will make them the center of attention while ignoring their emotions since the narcissist needs more inventory.

These people were frequently raised with the expectation that they would change a domestic situation, such as being estranged from their parents or older relatives, being neglected by their parents, or having a relative who misuses drugs.

These people feel compelled to help others, even if it hurts their physical or mental health. Narcissists seize on this, figuring that as long as their partner needs to mend their damaged character, they will always be in command.

#9 Laziness

Narcissists are always looking for situations in which they may exert complete control. They require a flexible partner in a relationship who is only interested in the outcome. Similarly, narcissists seek appreciation and acknowledgment for taking charge of the relationship.

#10 Compassion

Victimizers want to target those who pardon regularly and efficiently. They must understand that a bouquet and a remorse statement are all required to win back their partner's tremendous favor.

Since narcissists are unlikely to alter their destructive behaviors, a genuinely sympathetic partner is necessary for the relationship to succeed.

What Kind of Feeling Does a Narcissist Want in a Relationship?

Given the amount of time and work that goes into maintaining a relationship, it is difficult to understand why a self-centered narcissist would go through with it.

They don't require a relationship; they always think an opportunity will make them feel better about themselves. These are some constrictive ideals narcissists seek while they are with someone.

Feel strong

The sense of power that narcissists experience is among their most firmly rooted emotions. They are sure that they should establish the rules and conditions for living.

They should be regarded as the dominant force in a relationship. If you challenge them in any way, you've damaged their pride permanently and are likely to be eliminated.

Feel Important Compared to You

A narcissist finds nothing more irritating than someone controlling them. This makes them awkward because they can't be with someone who makes them appear harmful, but they can also avoid somebody who might steal the show.

Narcissists should negotiate a reasonable compromise with a spouse, so they can feel superior to you without feeling out of your league.

Feel Noticeable

From their vantage point, it appears as though the world doesn't recognize the narcissist's fantastic talent.

There will never be enough praise for what a narcissist does, whether it be for their gorgeous looks, how they are successful in their work, or something as simple as how they planned a dinner.

When their partner notices what they're willing to accomplish and bestows praise on them, narcissists cherish it.

Feel Fearful

Narcissists are filled with excessive self-confidence and require their partners to feel the same level of adoration for them.

Additionally, they require their partner to express their affection entirely whenever they are together, especially while another person is nearby.

Narcissists think everyone should be able to tell their partner like the ground they walk on.

Feeling in charge

Narcism's defining characteristic is the desire to feel in control constantly.

Because of their inner fragility, narcissists are dangerous people who can explode anytime if they feel threatened.

As a result, narcissists are much friendlier (and easier to be around) when they perceive themselves as in command. When they are associated with someone they have some control over, they are also happier.

How narcissists behave after a relationship ends

The one constant in a relationship with a narcissist is that it will end. A narcissist will always feel exhausted on their inventory source eventually, regardless of what that finishing looks like or how long it lasts.

The majority of narcissistic relationships end with a whimper rather than a boom. Before finalizing a friendship, a narcissist will belittle you for weeks or even months.

They want to convince themselves that you aren't worth sticking close to them, and they think you should recognize how little you've grown to mean to them. This period frequently includes offenses and extreme control.

After a period of debasement, the narcissist will get rid of their spouse, end their relationship, and carry on. This frequently means that they have found another source of supplies and are no longer dependent on their relationship. Tragically, if their new stock source fails, they could have to turn to their former partner at some point shortly.

CHAPTER THREE

Identifying narcissism

Narcissistic personality disorder (NPD): What is it?

In our selfie-obsessed, celebrity-driven world, the term "narcissist" is frequently used to describe someone who seems excessively vain or full of themselves. However, narcissism does not imply confidence psychologically, not certainty that can be verified. To put it more accurately, those who suffer from a narcissistic personality disorder (NPD) are enamored with a romanticized, conceited image of themselves. They are also undeniably drawn to this expanded mental self-portrait because it protects them from intense feelings of vulnerability. However, putting up their delusions of grandeur requires a lot of work, which is where the damaged minds and acting styles come in.

Narcissistic personality disorder includes:

- Arrogance.
- Pompous reasoning and behavior.
- Having no regard for people or no empathy.
- An irrational need for respect.

Others usually view people with NPD as demanding, arrogant, cunning, small-minded, and presumptuous. Every area of the narcissist's life—from work and relationships to relationships with family and romantic partners—displays this point of view and way of operating.

Narcissistic personality disorder patients are generally resistant to altering their behavior, even when it is causing them problems. They tend to blame others for the problem. They are also susceptible and take seriously even minor reactions, disagreements, or perceived slights, which they perceive as personal assaults. It's frequently more effortless for those around the narcissist to comply with their demands to avoid the cold and rage. However, by being more knowledgeable about narcissistic personality disorder, you may be able to spot narcissists regularly, defend yourself against their oppressive behaviors, and establish stronger boundaries.

Narcissistic personality disorder symptoms

An inflated feeling of importance

The main characteristic of narcissism is grandiosity. Affectedness is a silly sense of dominance distinct from self-importance or vanity. Narcissists acknowledge that they are "special" or one of a kind and that only extraordinary people can understand them. They are also perfect for anything typical. They need to connect to other high-status people, places, and things.

Narcissists also believe they are superior to everyone else and demand praise in this manner, even though they never genuinely deserve it. They usually exaggerate or even lie about their abilities and talents. Additionally, if they talk about their relationships or their work, all they talk about is how much they offer, how great they are, and how lucky the people in their lives are to have them. Everybody else is, at best, a supporting actor because they are undeniable stars.

Lives in a dream world that supports their grandiose delusions

Narcissists live in a dreamland created by bending, self-double dealing, and strange reasoning since reality doesn't support their arrogant view of themselves. To feel unique and in command, they turn to self-commending visions of boundless success, power, magnificence, appeal, and ideal love. The realities and conclusions that contradict them are ignored or rationalized since these fantasies protect individuals from feelings of interior emptiness and shame. The egomaniac's forsaking of fact is met with excessive protectiveness and even rage, so people around them must learn how to move carefully around their forsaking of fact.

Needs constant praise and affection

A narcissist's sense of superiority is like an inflatable that steadily loses air if it doesn't receive frequent affirmation and praise. An occasional compliment is insufficient. Narcissists surround themselves with people who will take special care of their compulsive desire for confirmation because they need constant nourishment for their inner selves. These connections are pretty unevenly distributed. Everything is always about how the narcissist's admirer can support them, never the other way around. Furthermore, the narcissist views any interruption or diminution in the admirer's consideration and praise as treachery.

A propensity for selfishness

Narcissists believe they are exceptional; thus, they demand admiration from others. They think that they should be able to obtain anything they want. They also assume that everyone around them acts according to their every whim and urge. Their primary value is that. If you don't anticipate and resolve all of their problems, you are useless. Additionally, if you dare to disagree with their decision or "childishly" ask for something in response, prepare to face wrath, shock, or rejection.

Uses others without being accountable or ashamed

The ability to relate to the feelings of others or to imagine other people's viewpoints is something that narcissists never develop. They ultimately require compassion. They view everyone around them as tools to satiate their desires in various ways. They, therefore, do not consider overusing others to complete their closures. Sometimes this double-dealing in relationships is motivated by revenge, but most of the time, it is not. Narcissists don't consider the implications of their behavior for other people. Additionally, even if you draw attention to it, they still won't understand it fully. They know their needs better than anything else.

Narcissists feel compromised whenever they encounter someone who appears to have what they need, incredibly confident and well-known. They do their best to criticize, frighten, threaten, or put down others. Additionally, those who do not grovel to them or who in any way confront them compromise them. Hatred is their means of defense. The best action is to put those people down to eliminate the threat and support their dangling inner selves. They might do it dismissively or carelessly to show how little the other person meant to them. Alternatively, they can launch an attack using insults, verbal abuse, harassment, and danger to force the other person back into line.

CHAPTER FOUR

How to recognize narcissists

Let's get one thing straight before you start self-diagnosing yourself or someone else with narcissistic personality disorder (NPD): There is a difference between someone having narcissistic traits and someone who has been diagnosed with NPD. For narcissistic personality disorder to be diagnosed, a person must exhibit behaviors with a getting-through pattern, which denotes that their behavior won't change. Even if it might not produce the desired results, it typically begins in their teens or mid-20s and continues throughout their lives.

What characteristics do narcissists seek in a partner?

It's hardly surprising that people with narcissistic personality disorder commonly use control and manipulation in love relationships.

Narcissists will consequently commonly look for partners who won't recognize that they are a reflecting pool and are incapable of seeing the gap in the relationship. For example, an objective is frequently someone who is anxious for admiration and willfully disregards warnings. So when this person, after going on a few dates, states, "I've never treasured somebody as I love you," no alarm goes out in their head that indicates, "Golly, it is pretty uncommon because I barely really know this individual."

Since sympathetic people are frequently aware of others' needs, becoming empathetic is also a common goal for narcissists. Furthermore, in specific ways, those who have experienced abuse or trauma in the past are also intensely targeted since when we endure gruesome encounters, we lose our ability to fend off new repressive situations.

Do narcissists recognize their narcissism?

The majority of the time, narcissists are either unaware of their condition or receive poor treatment if they are.

Narcissists lack awareness and comprehension; hence, they cannot see that they are a problem. If you disagree with them, they will distract you, humiliate and persuade you, or threaten you into helping them and play the victim.

Narcissists won't claim to be a part of any problem; instead, they'll use things you've said or done against you to manipulate you and convince you that the problem is with you.

Narcissists lack mindfulness; therefore, you may expect to be manipulated and gaslighted. They will gradually push against your boundaries until you yield to their demands.

Narcissists lack mindfulness; therefore, you may expect to be manipulated and gaslighted. They will gradually push against your boundaries till you fully concur with what they require.

Aware and unaware narcissists exist.

Most narcissists are unaware of their condition. They unintentionally behave egotistically or look for ways to justify their behavior. Additionally, a significant portion of their selfish behaviors is intuitive.

For example, a narcissist who isn't aware of their behavior wouldn't think, "I know, I'll threaten that person at work, so they won't have the solidarity to promote that promotion beyond me."

Assuming everything else is equal, their narcissism compels them to criticize what they accomplish naturally. Then complain to their employers and demean them in front of others. The narcissist believes that they are doing the right thing by discovering terrible work rehearsals. They also fail to recognize the benefits they receive because they think it will be beneficial in the long run.

Some narcissists, however, genuinely are aware of their condition. On the other hand, if they are unaware of the phrase, they are aware that they are cunning and manipulative.

These cognizant narcissists are less frequent. They are usually more intelligent and deliberately scheme and plan rather than retort and justify. Additionally, they will want to threaten someone with their closures.

Aware narcissists believe they are superior to weak, sympathetic people and enjoy taking advantage of them because they believe their deficiencies make them deserving of it. By citing phrases like "It's a cruel existence" and "survival of the fittest," they frequently justify it.

The behaviors of knowledgeable and unaware narcissists are remarkably comparable, despite the differences in approach. Said one does it consciously, and one does it unintentionally. In any case, their narcissistic behaviors are a result of their minds.

Every time they are tested, both will be legitimate and denied. Only the conscious narcissist will be more aware of what they're doing.

In rare circumstances, self-conscious narcissists are aware of their condition.

While some narcissists are aware of who they are, most are not. The category of cerebral narcissists includes those who are more self-aware and logical. Some might learn about this conflict and comprehend how these traits represent them if they read a lot about psychology. However, they won't just give it to everyone. Furthermore, they get better at being narcissists due to their examination.

For instance, if their spouse accuses them of lacking sympathy, they can respond by claiming that they believe them to be slightly mentally unstable. They think this explanation will cover up the fact that they are narcissists, which is their real problem.

They may accept or reject this reality if they are formally diagnosed with narcissistic personality disorder, a rare occurrence. They might also know if a relative tries to tell them, just in case.

However, they will typically deny these "accusations."

Most narcissists won't admit to having any faults.

Narcissists won't hold themselves accountable for whatever mistakes they make. So how could they possibly have ever admitted to being a narcissist? They believe themselves to be admirable people. They are protected from thinking they are misbehaving by their inner selves. They do not acknowledge responsibility for their deeds.

In the unlikely event that they damage someone else, they will blame the victim rather than express regret. They won't say sorry unless something unusual happens, like when someone is about to leave them. By that point, they will say anything and everything to prevent the person from going.

Anyone who can't help but disagree with them or raise doubt about them becomes their enemy. Additionally, they will eliminate that "enemy" to protect their reputation. Whether or not they had only recently expressed their love for that person.

Finally, narcissists' refusal to acknowledge their concerns is the root of their problems. They would be able to grow and work on themselves like a strong person if they could accept this apparent reality. However, they are tight because they can't admit to inappropriate activity. They don't act like ordinary adults because of it, which hinders their personal growth.

They refuse to try and accept it as accurate and reject it themselves.

Although each person is different, narcissists typically know they are tricky or even "seeking trouble." However, they don't have a quiet voice about it, at least not one that lasts, do they?

Additionally, it makes sense that they are willfully ignorant and even deceive themselves about who they are, given how unreliable and outright liars they can be. They, therefore, have their defenses that they employ to make it "OK," even though they may be aware that they are planning and completing tasks clandestinely.

If it does, what does it matter to them if it makes them feel better? Again, the moral dilemma

Therefore, even while many narcissists may not grasp what narcissism is, as more people become accustomed to how this problem exists explicitly, a narcissist probably wouldn't consider that it could apply to them unless they were expressly told it did.

After being told outright that they are a narcissist, their answer is frequently to refuse outrageously. Not only do they lie about it to everyone around them, but they also make an effort to fight back and label their victims as narcissists.

They also refuse to try and accept it as accurate and deny it to themselves.

However, once it was said, they might have realized there might be some truth. Additionally, if they allow themselves to think deeply about things, they might try to own up to their identity rather than for someone else.

Tragically, regardless of whether they reached that conclusion by admitting they were narcissists, they typically wouldn't change their methods. Narcissists are unchangeable.

Someone narcissistic at work

In the workplace, narcissists essentially make others depressed, which frequently leads to those workers exhibiting healthy worker syndrome and moving their work to another association, either because they are unable to or reluctant to express the issue or because they believe that HR or managers won't pay attention to or follow up on their nominations. Psychologists and HR companies understand and report narcissism and personality disorders in the workplace to a certain extent. Although narcissistic traits—misrepresented identity significance, a strong need for respect, a lack of empathy, and the desire for oppressive control over others—contradict positive character traits at work (such as inclusion, transparency, and sharing), narcissists frequently value promotion. Unlucky pioneers want deference, exhibit showy self-conviction, refuse to accept analysis, lack empathy, move indecisively, and receive lousy guidance. However, many narcissists hold potent positions, maybe mainly due to their brutal earnestness and world-building. Narcissism is unmistakably linked to counterproductive behaviors in the workplace, such as initiating reports, harming and disparaging other people's efforts, animosity, squandering other employees' time, and going against group dynamics. Employee raters who are knowledgeable and well-prepared can initially assess narcissists more effectively.

A narcissistic spectrum exists. A high spectrum score is primarily supported by: - An individual's identity significance that exceeds the norm or what may be perceived as acceptable by others. Lack of empathy for others Inability to comprehend the value of analysis (as it probably flattens their identity significance and uncommonness) Use other people's goodwill to maintain their idealized view of oneself as the dominant force (the so-called self-absorbed supply). This is necessary for veneration and might take the form of boasting, exaggerating successes, or pursuing high office. Expect to be viewed as better and compete vigorously against places that will manage the expense of that perception. Focusing on and emphasizing purely selfish traits, such as beauty, success, sexual prowess, and similar characteristics, dominates conversations and ignore opposing viewpoints. Condescending manner of conduct jealous of a few and uneasy in their organization Insist on having and displaying the best of everything, including your house, office, car, phone, wealth, and accomplice.

CHAPTER FIVE

How long does narcissism take to overcome?

It can be challenging to go over the trauma bond that narcissistic abuse caused. It's a refreshing endeavor that takes time, energy, and effort.

How long does it take to overcome narcissistic abuse, though?

This is a query that every victim asks. It's reasonable to wonder when you will ever arrive because you are right there, fighting for months or even years, and you haven't fully recovered.

Before anything else, you must be aware of a particular something. Before recovery, there is still a long way to go, so don't hold out hope for immediate miracles.

Considering everything, you will need a lot of time, work, and energy to undo the damage your narcissistic abuser did to your mental health and character. Even so, it might be completed with the correct social support system.

When you ask Ph.D. experts how long it often takes a victim of narcissistic abuse to heal, they will say that the average healing time is between twelve and eighteen months.

In any case, they will also draw their attention to the fact that each victim goes through a specific journeying process.

Disavowal

You learn about narcissistic and toxic people, and you become aware that there is such a thing as narcissistic abuse. In any event, you are convinced that this cannot happen to you, just like the rest of the world.

Similarly, you typically dismiss anything you're experiencing right away. You effectively refuse to admit that you are a survivor of narcissistic abuse.

All the warnings are present, but you keep convincing yourself that you're not seeing them. Maybe you're not telling the truth. It's possible that your abuser is not genuinely appalling in the larger scheme.

You may be just being overly sensitive.

It seems inconceivable that you would have spent this much time and effort with someone so evil and cunning. The indicators would have been apparent previously.

Nothing changes, even when your closest friends and family members are trying to help you open your eyes.

It doesn't help that your egotist keeps gaslighting you and portraying you as the insane one.

Regardless of the rejection, this stage is unquestionably remarkable. It suggests that you've finally started reflecting on and reevaluating your narcissistic relationship.

This marks the start of a more extensive journey, your complex and drawn-out journey of repair. But because it represents some growth, this is important.

Finally, you've gotten out of the dead zone and started moving forward.

Guilt

You need to be aware of something while thinking about how long it takes to heal from narcissistic abuse.

With this healing process, there are both highs and lows.

You could assume that acknowledgment should occur immediately after forswearing. Despite this, though, things don't always operate in a clear-cut manner.

After the initial stage, you start to feel sorry, to be honest. You initially feel guilty for accusing your lover of being a narcissist.

Sooner or later, when you learn more about narcissistic personality traits and realize that your partner exhibits the bulk of them, you also experience guilt.

You are under siege from guilt on many fronts. You find it difficult to comprehend why you would interact with such a toxic sociopath.

Why didn't you notice the symptoms earlier? How could you possibly have been so stupid as to ignore the apparent warnings?

Above all, how is it possible that you have maintained a close relationship with this person for such a long time? When did you lose your self-respect?

How could you have stood by and let them treat you in this manner for so long? Did you become lost?

These are the thoughts you're having. You decide to take the opposite action rather than blaming your abuser entirely because they are the only ones who deserve to be held accountable.

You've been so thoroughly brainwashed that you even blame yourself for being their victim.

This is another attempt on the part of your mind to forgive them of all responsibility, though you won't immediately know it.

Outrage

The next stage also includes negative emotions, with outrage as the dominant.

It's much easier for you to be enraged when you're angry at your abuser, mad at yourself for choosing them and for being with them, and angry at the universe for putting you in this situation because you're not yet ready to handle your anger and everything you've been through.

It's much easier to admit that you're angry than to admit that you've been hurt and crushed.

One can even say that you can't stand your abuser right now. You think they ought to encounter the same difficulties that you did.

You have to make amends. You plan your revenge, and the main thing that calms you down is picturing them suffering emotionally.

The majority of victims don't significantly change anything with this. However, they consider retaliation because it serves as their defense weapon.

You think this is the best way to reclaim your respect and confidence. The only way you can stop feeling embarrassed is for the abuser to go through what you did.

Indeed, believe me when I say that anger is never preferable to pity. You seem to have a strong bond with your narcissist.

Additionally, vengeance won't repair your broken heart. It might restore your damaged self-image, but it won't magically heal all of your long-standing wounds.

Dealing

The phase known as dealing follows after anger, which is probably the last thing you anticipate when you try to figure out how long it takes to recover from narcissistic abuse.

Don't decide to do all in your power to harm your victimizer up until this point. You despised them and resolved never to revisit them.

In any case, you probably already knew this, but the reality is different. Since you still have a lot of flexibility, your repeated lapses in trust serve as the best evidence of your vulnerability.

Even though it's unexpected, you start to talk to yourself about how you might help your narcissist.

Even though you try to detach yourself from it, there is no longer any underlying fury. Instead, faith in the other person's ability to change, your ability to help them, and the possibility that your narcissistic relationship might be salvaged emerges.

You reflect on all the ambiguities. You consider your narcissist's potential and all they could become in the unlikely event that they agree to undergo a few minor character modifications.

You'll most likely resume communication with your abuser during this period. Typically, this doesn't help with handling your recovery.

Keeping in mind that these poisoned individuals are competent controllers and that they are expected to attempt to modify the course of events is your best course of action.

It's conceivable that your abuser will make a sincere effort to identify as your victim.

You won't ever be able to trust them on a conscious level. However, you will need to allow them back into your life when it matters, so you should respect their motivations.

The period of no interaction

I won't lie to you; this will probably be the most challenging part of your recovery from the long marathon.

This is your first physical action against your narcissist; all previous ones are inside your thoughts and emotions.

Break all links and refrain from communicating with your victim when you need to leave an abusive relationship and are unsure how long it will take you to recover from narcissistic abuse.

Please recognize that this person has a severe narcissistic personality problem, but remember to be friendly with them.

There is no acculturated way to do this; therefore, I won't mislead you. You won't have the choice to politely explain to them why you need to leave and that you won't be seeing them again.

All you'll need to do is, as expected, put some distance between you and them. Block their virtual entertainment accounts, break off relationships with all of your close friends, and it will probably be necessary to change your phone number.

This will be more demanding if you have a toxic relationship that you need to continue co-nurturing with a narcissistic parent, a coworker, or a partner.

These are people you need to keep in touch with in some capacity.

If it's not too much bother, keep your correspondence with this co-parent or associate to matters of work or the kids and refrain from engaging in any other conversation.

However, if it's not too tricky, neglect your family obligations and relationships if we talk about a narcissistic parent.

Despite your blood connection, you can and should cut ties with them because you are an adult.

In either case, the key is to ignore the narcissist to the greatest extent possible.

Although I know you will probably want to argue with them and call them out on their behavior, trust me when I say it will not be successful.

Your response is a narcissistic supply. No matter what kind of reaction we're talking about, it doesn't matter; for their needs, it's sufficient to demonstrate that they have found a way to contact you.

It would be best if you pretended that they don't exist because of this. Make your victimizer's life as difficult as possible, and they will eventually give up on you.

That won't magically cure their NPD. Sadly, you can do little to stop them from moving on to their next victim.

Regaining your composure

Better days are ahead if you've completed the previous stage and you're progressively determining how long it will take you to recover from narcissistic abuse.

Finally, you can free yourself from the suffering this emotional abuse has caused you.

This is when you need to learn how to love yourself again. The stage at which you wish to take the lead and the stage that has to do with regaining your confidence.

It would be best if you gave yourself another chance. Work on yourself and, more importantly, keep yourself as busy as possible.

No, your narcissistic abuser won't magically vanish from your head; instead, you must decide to expel them.

Many narcissistic abuse victims lack the strength to endure all of this alone. People require an emotional support system that includes assistance from their friends, family, or knowledgeable professionals.

Please don't be afraid to seek assistance.

You're not helpless; after all, you're in charge of someone with a severe case of excessive narcissism, so it's only natural that you can't escape their control on your own.

Creating a new personality

Becoming new is one of the most challenging aspects of recovering from narcissistic abuse.

The character you had before you met your narcissistic ex was destroyed, and the trauma link you shared with them altered the physical manifestation of who you are.

So, it is the perfect time to rediscover the person you were before.

The truth is that this terrible experience will impact your mental health. Emotional wounds will eventually heal with time, but the scars will last forever.

No, I'm not saying you're broken or incapable of recovery; I'm just trying not to believe that you'll return to being the same person you were before this person entered your life.

But you need to develop a new personality that won't be dependent on your abuser but won't be a carbon copy of the one you had before they came around.

Do the math

Despite what you might believe, your narcissistic abuser is still very much present in your life and your emotions throughout this time.

There are still moments in time when you want to give up and when you have a glimmer of hope that your narcissistic ex will transform and become one of your ideal lovers.

In any event, you finally take off your rose-colored glasses at this point. You eventually start to see reality in its actual structure beyond this point.

You stop justifying your partner's harmful behavior. You stop justifying the narcissist abuse and stop blaming yourself for what happened.

You stop believing they'll develop into empaths or kind people.

You are aware of the negative consequences of their severe psychological instability, that they require help, and that you are unlikely to have a significant impact.

This reality check is unpleasant from the get-go. In the long run, nevertheless, it gives you freedom. You're finally set free from this person's bonds.

You are aware that their behaviors are unusual and that you shouldn't anticipate the same treatment from everyone around you.

This is added when you might start dating again, assuming we're talking about an ex-significant other you've been trying to avoid.

Your capacity for optimistic thinking is reawakened, and you suddenly realize there is cause for optimism.

In any event, I'll have to ask that you use extreme caution when rebound relationships. Because of how vulnerable you still are, you could easily be duped by someone's repeated attempts at affection.

Acknowledgment and forgiveness

When truth hits you square in the face, now is the time to admit it, make an excuse, and—most importantly—stop looking for the answer. You realize that you will never learn the information you seek.

The reason why all of this happened is not well explained, which is most significant.

At the same time, I don't remember you trying to take off from the same position again. Although you don't let it define you, you know that trying to get away from something part of you is pointless.

You expressly understand what absolution means. You still offer forgiveness after whatever you encounter.

Most importantly, you realize that you are neither insane nor stupid and that you can forgive yourself for all of your wrong choices as a whole.

64

Because the victim is never at fault, you were a victim. You admit your faults without allowing them to undermine your self-worth.

You finally discover a way to find the support necessary to defend your narcissistic abuser. Even if your life depended on it, you don't need them back; instead, you forgive them.

Right now, you're wise enough to understand that your bitterness and hatred only hurt you.

You realize that giving up anger and any lingering pessimism is the most excellent way to free yourself from this person's influence.

You start to distance yourself from them at this stage and successfully get rid of them.

Acquired knowledge

You frequently ignore what happens next while thinking about how long it takes to heal from narcissistic abuse.

You forget one crucial detail: the illustrations this self-centered relationship taught you.

Could you ever know that you're fully recovered till you realize that you've learned something from this horrible experience?

First and foremost, you'll learn how to take charge and start worrying about your financial and emotional well-being.

You'll become aware of your self-worth, participate in taking care of yourself, and learn how to love yourself more than anybody else.

Additionally, you'll build extraordinary amounts of confidence. You'll realize that you are the ideal companion and don't need anybody to depend on.

Above all, this connection will teach you the opposite of what love is. You'll learn to perceive things like control, love bombardment, and many tactics narcissists use to entice victims.

The hardship of this experience cannot be disputed. It is necessary, though, as it will give you a better sense of solidity.

CHAPTER SIX

How do I get rid of my narcissism?

The Best Approach to Quitting Being a Narcissist

The majority of narcissists might not be aware of their inclinations.

In any event, realizing that you might possess narcissistic qualities is a positive development, and being open to change is a genuine possibility.

Here are some constructive ways you can alter your behavior to make things better:

As demonstrated by (at least five) of the following, narcissism is an unavoidable example of vainglory (in fantasy or action), demand for reverence, and absence of compassion, commencing by early adulthood and evident in diverse settings:

- Possesses a vain identity significance (e.g., misrepresents accomplishments and gifts, hopes to be perceived as predominant without comparable achievements).
- Is consumed by fantasies of unbounded success, strength, brilliance, magnificence, or ideal love.
- He accepts that the person is "special" and novel and that they must be perceived by, or should interact with, other distinctive or eminent people (or establishments).
- Demands excessive praise.
- Has a propensity for narcissism, as evidenced by their unbelievable expectations for exceptional treatment or their programming of behavior to support those expectations.
- Is erratic in relationships (for example, exploits others to accomplish their closures).

- Lacks compassion: struggles to understand or empathize with the needs and sentiments of others.
- Constantly desires others or acknowledges that others are envious of the subject.
- Displays arrogant, conceited, or self-important behaviors or viewpoints.

General psychotherapy is justified if the patient possesses at least 5 of these traits.

If by some lucky coincidence, there are a few highlights, psychotherapy can also address them. The traits typically last for a very long time and are not frequently noticed by the person by themselves.

When someone who frequently considers a narcissist mentions some of these traits, they are either rejected or taken to mean that this is how everyone is. This way, altering or eliminating these traits is complicated.

In the off case that the person isn't receiving treatment, here are some suggestions:

1. Draw attention to whether the person's perspective on his accomplishments is incorrect and how their goals should be determined. For instance, if you are the narcissist's employer, specify the precise tasks that must be completed and how to perform them, as shown with careful development.

2. Realize that having a casual relationship with someone of great rank won't instantly elevate you to their level of respect or give you access to their resources. It takes perseverance and hard work.

3. If a person becomes disheartened, you can suggest that they feel insulted and, shockingly, angered since they didn't receive the continual admiration they crave.

4. While it may be difficult for someone without compassion to understand someone else's lack of empathy, efforts can be made to emphasize that

people may have feelings that are different from their own. Consequently, learning about their attitudes and opinions is wise. In addition, mindsets are shifting as people begin to recognize that everyone is different in some way and deserves respect and consideration.

5. A challenging but excellent starting point is teaching the narcissist to painstakingly listen to others without interruption and then rephrase what has been said.

6. The topic of envy is exceptionally delicate. The narcissist's feelings of jealousy, disgrace, disappointment, or insecurity should be able to be tenderly soothed by being related to them in some way.

7. Haughtiness is incredibly difficult to overcome since the person feels inadequate and mediocre, and their arrogant demeanor serves as a defense. If the person doesn't feel condemned but rather

targeted, being aware of these feelings could help them let go of their watchman.

In general, it could seem strange, yet the narcissist needs a lot of empathy without condemnation. The narcissist can unintentionally feel empty inside, having missed out on early developmental affection and support, or have been erroneously exposed, delivering their sense of pretentiousness and illegitimate power.

To this end, psychological health professionals who are just incredibly prepared can stop someone from becoming a narcissist through a lengthy treatment. This person deserves a lot of respect and compassion even if they shouldn't be considered evil. They are suffering emotionally.

The problem is that most narcissists attempt to hide their ignorance, rationalize their actions, or are even prodded into acting egotistically by others who use the term. Nothing is known.

Contrary to popular belief, narcissistic people overcompensate for lack of confidence and use 'pain-avoidance' strategies. Often, a narcissist is unaware of this truth.

It's a maladaptive guard feature that keeps a strategic distance from suffering and engages in excessive self-venture. They bolster themselves with justifications and evidence because they are known for having weak emotional fortitude.

A narcissist is unprepared to witness someone else's annoyance or complaint since he doesn't allow himself to feel helpless within. There can be a history of trauma, agony, or feelings of inadequacy from high school or earlier in life.

It makes sense that there could be overbearing guardians as well. People in a cozy relationship with a narcissist typically suffer because their needs are disregarded.

As a narcissist, you can help yourself by doing the following:

1. Knowing the likelihood that there will be at least two correct answers

They frequently assume that if I am sure I am right, the other person must be mistaken, yet it is possible to have at least two accurate answers depending on the viewpoint.

For instance, it is feasible that yoga, running, or going to an exercise facility might be the most acceptable kind of physical activity. Each person might consider any of these responses to be accurate.

2. Embrace feedback.

Get cryptic feedback from friends and family on any adjustments you've made or any problems others are having with you so you can examine your conduct.

becoming more aware of the present moment

Instead of approaching every day, individual, and scenario with bias, take a stand by listening to what people have to say.

3. Recognize old injuries

Try to determine whether you haven't experienced pain or trauma recently or in the past.

4. Empathy

Although it is a skill that may be learned, empathy is not an intrinsic ideal. You may grow your empathy for yourself and other people.

Being narcissistic allows your frailty and desire for acceptance to overpower other people's needs.

Ten things are anticipated to recover from self-indulgence. The individual's undeniable need...

- Keep in mind that they are narcissistic or, at the very least, act in selfish ways.

- Admit that you are one or possess qualities of one.
- Want to alter.
- Seek assistance; the ordinary person cannot complete the task alone.
- Develop new skills and use them regularly.
- Alter their worldviews.
- Treat their injuries.
- Help them alter their erroneous perceptions and incorrect beliefs about the world, other people, and themselves.
- Put their interests first; excuse both themselves and other people for any transgressions.

CHAPTER SEVEN

Does narcissistic personality disorder run in the family?

Narcissistic personality disorder: What is its cause?

The environment during childhood and adolescence may have a significant role in the development of NPD, although genetics may also play a role.

The complex personality illness known as a narcissistic personality disorder (NPD) is frequently misunderstood. When thinking about NPD, traits like an arrogant identity, a strong need for deference, and difficulty relating come to mind.

A person with NPD may first come across as charming and assured. While these endearing qualities may seem a given, they frequently conceal uncertainties rather than emanating from a place of confidence.

If you have NPD, you may be particularly sensitive to criticism or strongly react to offensive speech or behaviors.

A narcissistic personality disorder is almost definitely caused by genetics, environmental factors (including the connection between the child and parents), and environmental factors.

What environmental factors contribute to NPD?

Culture and parenting are environmental factors that may contribute to the development of narcissistic personality disorder.

Negative adolescent experiences, such as being rejected or reprimanded by parents, might contribute to NPD in adults. Moreover, NPD could also be brought on by parents recognizing you too much.

According to parenting and NPD research, different caring philosophies and narcissistic traits in adult children are related.

Anyhow, there isn't "one" loving behavior that consistently fosters narcissism.

A confluence of various nurturing philosophies and additional contributing factors (such as heredity) may result in NPD.

Generally speaking, these nurturing qualities are linked to higher degrees of narcissism in children:

1. Helicopter parenting or excessive protection

Lack of warmth; drawing too few or loose boundaries (intolerance); praise that elevates perfection or makes irrational assumptions (overvaluation); abuse or misuse

One study found that in young adults, overprotection was associated with both susceptible and grandiose narcissism. Setting some boundaries was associated with sensitive narcissism, keeping in mind that excessive applause was linked to grandiosity.

What is the treatment for a narcissistic personality disorder?

A combination of therapy and medication treats most mental health disorders. In any case, medicines don't work for personality disorders like NPD. Drugs will be used to treat the side effects of any co-occurring conditions that may be present, assuming they are approved.

The best chances for recovery for those with narcissistic personality disorder are provided by programs that offer individual, group, and family therapy. Long-term treatment that is consistent and more vital can help people with NPD realize how their condition has hurt their lives and kept them from reaching their full potential. The assistance of friends, family, and loved ones can add context, profundity, and support to these acknowledgments.

Mental health therapists won't attack the issue openly or aggressively because narcissism is an organizing factor of personality for NPD victims. The therapeutic encounter should be brought closer with intention and attentiveness to avoiding driving the patient too far or too quickly.

In a collaborative effort, therapists and narcissistic patients will identify the viewpoints and behavioral patterns that add stress, difficulty, and disappointment to the patient's life. As the healing process progresses, therapists will encourage NPD patients to take positive action to increase the negative impact of their narcissistic symptoms, offering practical advice and direction to help them.

Therapists treating narcissistic patients should construct an environment where critical viewpoints are excluded, and the center is precisely arranged. This is important because a successful treatment approach can foster trust and facilitate a more fruitful dialogue between medical professionals and patients.

Programs of evidence-based therapy for people with narcissistic personality disorder frequently include:

1. Behavioral and cognitive treatment. Victims of narcissistic personality disorder might learn how to replace arrogant and warped views with additional constructive and realistic ones through several CBT sessions.

2. Psychodynamic counseling. Patients with NPD will go into the depths of their past interactions during psychodynamic treatment sessions, evaluate the effects of risky relationships on their life, and examine naive assumptions about themselves and others that support narcissistic attitudes.

3. Family counseling. As much as it affects individuals, narcissistic behavior also impacts families. Involving friends and family in the healing and recovery process can help NPD sufferers see the actual effects of their selfish behavior.

Printed in Great Britain
by Amazon

17084903R00054